Lessons in Accountability
from My Father
Behavior
Responsible
Actions
Results
TRUST
LOYALTY
CONFIDENCE
Written by: Samtra K. Devard
Illustrations: Leroy Grayson
Published by: Jazzy Kitty Publications

Lessons in Accountability from My Father

By Samtra K. Devard

Cover Design by Leroy Grayson

Logo Designs by Leroy Grayson

Editor: Anelda L. Attaway

ISBN 978-1-954425-62-0

Library of Congress Control Number: 2022919757

ACKNOWLEDGMENTS

I want to acknowledge my husband, Leonard Devard and our three children, who share me with the things I am called to lend my time and talent to. Thank you for your love and your support.

DEDICATION

This book is dedicated to my father, Samuel Giles – a man of courage and conviction. He believed in personal responsibility and especially accountability. He lived an honorable life and served his family, friends, community, and God. I remember the last sermon my Dad and I attended together at our church. It was based on Luke 12:48 (NLT):

"But someone who does not know and then does something wrong will be punished only lightly. When someone has been given much, much will be required in return; and when someone has been entrusted with much, even more, will be required."

My father held himself accountable and as well as those around him. My Dad made sure I knew what was right and held me accountable for it – just as God does.

My father gave me so much – he met my needs (not necessarily all of my wants). He shaped my soul; he planted seeds in my spirit that are beginning to bear fruit. My earthly father did everything my Heavenly Father is now doing in me. I thank God for my Dad.

.

LESSONS IN HIS WORDS

Things He Used to Say

- You can do anything you put your mind to.

- Anything another person can do, you can do.

- Anything worth having will be harder to get.

- Make something of yourself.

- Fun is short-lived.

- It's the same distance from my house as it is to yours.

- You will have very few friends in life; the rest are only acquaintances. Know the difference.

- You will never be good at keeping house; hire a maid.

- Remember, no one has to like you but demand that they respect you.

- Lump is a little heavy on the gas.

- Boys and books don't mix.

- It would be easy to say yes. Knowing when to say no is my responsibility to you as a parent.

- I don't care if you think I'm hard, overprotective, or strict. I am.

- I don't care what someone else is doing – we are going to do what is right.
- Don't come to me with "dumb" stuff.
- Never lie to me.
- I will always tell you the truth – even when you don't want to hear it.
- I have no time for simple-minded people.

LESSONS IN HIS LIVING
Things He Used to Do

- My father always called and visited his mother.

- My father routinely visited other relatives.

- My father would readily share what he had with others.

- If my father had it to give – he'd give it. ("It" being time, money, advice, a kick-in-the-butt)

- My father would take the time to talk to you, listen, and explain things – especially children.

- My father required me to do well in school.

- My father took the time to get involved in my activities and my life.

- My father would not ever let anyone disrespect him or those he loved.

- My father had a temper but knew when it needed to be unleashed.

- My father would not allow me to be exposed to things that were in conflict with his sense of wrong.

- My father never *said* "I love you" – he *showed* me.

- My father was not afraid to let me see him cry when he lost his mother.
- My father lived with no regrets.
- My father found Jesus Christ and was saved.

TABLE OF CONTENTS

TABLE OF CONTENTS

TABLE OF CONTENTS

TABLE OF CONTENTS

TABLE OF CONTENTS

INTRODUCTION

This journey to share my father with the world began on Father's Day, 2005. After having gone through several rough days, I began reflecting on the calm that my father used to bring to my life. The quiet confidence of his mere presence just made everything all right – no matter what it was.

Losing my father was one of the greatest losses that I have ever experienced. His short battle with cancer was a journey of preparation for living my life without him. We talked so much during his illness – so much more than we had before. And trust me, my father and I talked a lot! There was so much to say, and it felt like it was so little time to say it. But my heart is glad to know that all that needed to be said had actually been said already – throughout my entire life. He didn't need to tell me he loved me. I knew it. He didn't need to tell me how proud he was of me. I knew it. He didn't need to say anything that validated my existence. I knew I belonged.

My father actually needed me to know that every decision he ever made since I was born was what he believed to be the best he knew to do at the time.

He said, "You may have thought I was hard."

I stopped him – "Yes, you were, but I was the better for it."

He said, "You may have thought I was overprotective." I stopped him again – "Yes, you were, but I always knew you were looking out for me."

What was profound was that at a mere 22 years of age, I had matured enough to know how great of a father that I had. I had known to appreciate all that we had shared. I knew our relationship was special.

My father's final days were turbulent. My mother and I made daily treks to the hospital and spent our entire days with him, grateful to have each and every moment with him. So, in his final moments, he held on... because he knew we'd be there. As we reached his room, our eyes locked. He looked at me so deeply as if to say, 'you're okay! I'm going on now.' His short battle with cancer culminated in his final moments being the most profound exchange of acceptance that a father and daughter could have. He was understood and appreciated. I was at peace that he was proud of the person I had become – the person he molded. He then closed his eyes. Forever.

So, this Father's Day – I wanted to pay tribute to him by sharing with the world all the wisdom that I was fortunate to be given during our years together.

On the 16th anniversary of my father's passing, Mr. Samuel Giles, for whom my firstborn son and I were named, share with the world – **Lessons in Accountability from My Father.**

You can do anything you put your mind to.

It was wonderful to have someone tell you daily that you can do anything. And what is more wonderful, I believed it. There was my Dad cheering me on each and every thing I set out to do. Telling me I can do it. I know you can. Even when I met with a challenge or two, there he was with words of wisdom.

I remember when my father was teaching me to drive. He was the hardest teacher. He fussed. He chastised. He quite frankly got on my nerves. One time he made me so frustrated that I pulled the car over to the side of the road.

I said, "That's it. I don't want to know how to drive."

He said, "Really?"

I said, "Yeah."

He said, "You're going to give up on something you have always wanted to do simply because it's hard."

"No, I'm not going to let you give up. Start the car."

I did. And that was that.

Anything another person can do, you can do.

How empowering to know that you can do anything someone else has done or is doing. So many people recount my father telling them this. So many people believed him and took charge of their lives. For me, I found the ability to persevere in knowing that whatever I was attempting had been done. So therefore, why wouldn't I be able to do it too?

Anything worth having will be harder to get.

This was surprising for me because much of what you pick up as a young person is that things are easy. You see, movie stars, sports heroes, and hip-hop artists all make it look easy. But my father tried to let me know as early as he could that it won't be easy – but it is still worth doing.

LESSON FOUR

Make something of yourself.

My father made it clear at every opportunity that he had expectations of me. He had expectations that I do something with my life. He never cared what I was striving to be, just that I strive to do something honorable. He also pressed upon me to do whatever I do to the best of my ability. Some parents make demands that their children be a doctor or lawyer or follow in their footsteps. My father never got into any of that. Just do something – which hopefully enables you to support yourself.

Fun is short-lived.

Out of all the stuff that my father used to say, much of it pretty abstract for a growing girl in her teens, this lesson was most disappointing. I used to ask him if fun and happiness don't last – what's the point? I don't truthfully know if he ever satisfied me with his answer. He used to say that's just life. But since becoming an adult – I have learned that no words have ever been more true. More importantly than knowing that fun doesn't last was his unspoken message of making sure that you are not aligning yourself with things that don't last. Things like the parties and the sophomoric good times are just drops of water in the ocean – they fade away so quickly and have no lasting impact on humanity. Being good to people, serving others, and honoring family are all things that he did in his life that lasted.

It's the same distance from my house as it is to yours.

My father visited his mother faithfully. He always let her know by deed or word that he was thinking of her. My grandmother lived with my aunt – my father's sister. Usually, he would visit them at least once per week – purely out of respect for my grandmother. After my grandmother passed away, my father stopped visiting with the same frequency. One day my aunt confronted my father about why she hadn't seen him in so long, referencing that she used to see him every week. She was trying to chastise him for not coming to visit. His answer was short and sweet, and I never forgot it that he said, "It's the same distance from my house to yours." Without having to say any more – my father made it very clear that she had no right to expect anything more than she was willing to do herself. She hadn't seen him, but that was a two-way street, and she needed to recognize her responsibility as well.

You will have very few friends in life; the rest are only acquaintances. Know the difference.

My father gave me so much wisdom; I quite frankly, didn't know what to do with it all. This lesson was to let me know that I will know a lot of people in my life. Don't give every one of them what should only be given to people who have shown themselves to be worthy of your heart.

"Friends are few," he said, "because not everyone will hold you in the same regard. Don't try to please everybody. Don't worry about something trivial or someone who is not treating you like they should."

You will never be good at keeping house; hire a maid.

My father knew me. And as I write this, I must confess these words are still true. But what I have neglected in these words is the validation that they bring. I may not be a good housekeeper, but I am still okay. He never said I wouldn't make a good wife or mother or that I wasn't a good daughter or person. This lesson was permission to accept that I have an area of weakness and that there is a way around it.

Remember, no one has to like you but demand that they respect you.

If there were one thing that my father took seriously, it would be respect for him. He tolerated no level of disrespect. Your correction and punishment would be swift and your education – long-lasting. I remember my father making this statement to the newest pastor of the church we attended. When my father fell ill, our pastor made regular visits with my father – whether it was to the hospital or our home. Our pastor was experiencing some dissension amongst our congregation and while my father rarely engaged in that kind of backbiting, he was often very aware of what went on around him. One thing that stood out for me was that I wasn't sure who was there to provide comfort to whom – our pastor to my father or my father to our pastor. It turned out that my father often provided our pastor with uplifting words rather than the reverse. I believe our pastor came to have his spirits lifted. After some major unrest, the pastor showed up as usual to give my father his communion. The pastor's heart seemed heavy. The pastor told a story that left him feeling down because it seemed like no one in the congregation liked him. My father told him point blank, so what. They don't have to like you. But you better make sure they respect you. You're not there to make friends; you're there to lead. So, lead! Wow. Pastor's eyes got wide. His shoulders lifted. It was an epiphany to him – and to me. Most leaders won't necessarily be liked. They're there to lead.

Lump is a little heavy on the gas.

I used to hear this statement more times than I count. Now, I proudly say the nickname my father had for me. It was "Lump." There I said it. For so long, I ran from that nickname. I felt diminished by it. I had (oops, have) a big forehead and the kids used to tease me. My father would call out Lump, and the kids would mock me and say Lumphead. I chuckle now, but back then, I cringed. Oh, how I would love to hear his booming voice saying Lump. But this lesson was about how I drive. I stuck it out. I eventually got my license. My father loved having me drive him around. In fact, often, he would just let me do all of the driving. As he got ill and was in and out of the hospital, I would drive my mother and I back and forth to visit him. He would tell her to watch out for Lump... she's a little heavy on the gas. But I mention this here not only as it relates to my driving, but also I'll use it as a metaphor for how I live my life. I'm a little heavy on the gas and often, I need to slow down. I take on more than I should. I often don't recognize my limits. I proceed too quickly before I have a chance to assess all of the risks. With age, I've gotten so much better at this. But there is certainly more room for improvement.

Boys and books don't mix.

As I got interested in boys... and boy was I interested, my father cautioned me at every turn not to let myself get too serious about any one boy. You'll be distracted from your studies, he warned. Back then, I thought I could do it all. Of course, I met someone with whom I just fell head over heels in love. As an aside, I eventually went on to marry this certain person and have three children with him – but I digress. Back while I was in school and in love, I will admit that I could not do both very well, and my grades slipped. I was pretty smart, so I had room for them to slide a little in high school. When I got to college, there was no room for them to get any lower. Occasionally, I think about how things might have been different in college if I weren't in love. Maybe C's could have been... who knows.

It would be easy to say yes. Knowing when to say no is my responsibility to you as a parent.

This little lesson sparked so much ire between my father and me. I would ask to do something that seemed harmless. Something that everyone else, I mean everyone else, was doing and he would say no. He said no to this and no to that. No, you can't go over to her house; her mother isn't home. No, you can't ride your bike around the corner; I can't see you. No, you can't go to the store with them; I don't even know if they have insurance on their car. No, you can't go to the party; I don't know their parents nor the kids that will be there. No, you can't date until you're 16; there'll be plenty of time for boys. I could go on and on and on. My father had no problem saying no to me. He never once compromised on his principles. He always wanted me to keep the right company, do the right things, and, most importantly, respect his answer. I obeyed but honestly, as a kid who couldn't do all that her friends could, I had a hard time with this. I would answer him if it's so hard, then just say yes, or it doesn't seem like you're having a hard time saying no – in my opinion. Having the gift of hindsight, so much of what he tried to shield me from made a difference in how my life turned out. Thankfully, I had the chance to let him know how much I appreciated his ability to say no.

I don't care if you think I'm hard, overprotective, or strict. I am.

This one speaks for itself.

I don't care what someone else is doing – we are going to do what is right.

This lesson and the one before it really get at the heart of who my father was. He knew who he was – he made no apologies for it. He knew what he believed to be right. He was never (I mean NEVER) swayed by peer pressure. He didn't care what anyone thought of him. He had his principles. There was never any cause to compromise them.

Don't come to me with "dumb" stuff.

My father expected you to be smart enough to approach him intelligently – meaning, he wanted to believe you had thought through what you needed to discuss with him and, more importantly, that you weren't trying to pull a fast one on him. This gets back to respect. I think he viewed this as asking to be spared the nonsense.

Never lie to me.

I made the mistake of lying to my father once. I got caught. Not a little *white lie*. Not a little *untruth*. This one was a whopper. My father dropped me off to visit my cousin, and she was planning to visit her boyfriend. My cousin was allowed to visit the houses of boys – something I was NOT allowed to do. I knew it. My cousin knew it. But we both decided we were going to do it anyway. She told her Mom; we were visiting a friend who lived around the corner. And I thought we could go and make it back before my father returned to pick me up. Well, he returned earlier than anyone expected. My aunt called my cousin's friend to ask us to come home, and she said we weren't there and that we hadn't been there. My aunt scoured the neighborhood looking for us, and we were nowhere to be found. Sad to say, but in this day and age, an AMBER Alert might have been activated for us. But back then the Sam-alert was activated, and he was getting upset. Eventually, we come strolling back. As we approached, I said to my cousin – that looks like your Mom standing there in the street. As we walked closer, indeed it was. My aunt cussed and she yelled out get your a** over here! She said my father was back, and they had been looking for us for hours. We said we were at my cousin's friend's house; my aunt cut that lie short and said that's a d*** lie. My father whisked me into our car and took me home and boy was I in for it. He seemed calm for him. Which I should have been smart enough to know was a warning sign. He asked me where we were, and I tried to make up some story, but he told me straight out – you were not anywhere to be found. Everybody looked in every possible place for you. All the other kids and their parents looked, and you weren't there. Where were you? I finally realized that I had to come clean. I told him we had gone to my cousin's boyfriend's house. That's when the volcano erupted. I had never seen my father so angry. I assured him nothing happened. That my cousin and her boyfriend had engaged in nothing wrong, blah, blah... his slap stopped me cold. He asked me why did I choose to lie to him? And then came the honesty – too little, too late. I told him I had lied because I didn't think he would have approved of me going, and I wanted to go. This was blatant disrespect for the rules. He asked me again why did I choose to lie to him? I told him – I didn't want to get in trouble. And boy, was I in trouble. He explained to me about why we have rules. He told me how worried he was something had happened to the both of us. He told me how unfair it was to my aunt to have violated his trust in her. He told me I needed to apologize to my aunt for lying to her. I left that episode feeling so low. It was not only because of how much trouble I found myself in; I felt horrible because I had really disappointed my father. I knew I never wanted to have him feel about me the way he did that day – I never forgot it.

I will always tell you the truth – even when you don't want to hear it.

The truth, I mean here, is constructive criticism. My father didn't waste time with little white lies that served no purpose. When you truly love someone and have their best interests at heart, you will tell them what they need to hear. He used to say, how can you trust someone who would lie to you about the little things? You won't be able to trust them with your heart – when it really matters. Sometimes it would be tough to hear that you didn't get something because you didn't try hard enough or that cake recipe I tried didn't turn out quite right; but how do you get better if someone who loves you can't whisper in your ear something that could help you improve.

LESSON EIGHTEEN

I have no time for simple-minded people.

This lesson really speaks for itself, but I need to say something here. My father always had a minute for anyone who needed his advice or his encouragement. But if it became apparent to him that you weren't really interested in doing what was right or taking responsibility for yourself and the things you did – then he would be done talking. He didn't like wasting time trying to convince you to change; you had to want to change.

LESSON NINETEEN

My father always called and visited his mother.

I never realized while I was young how important doing this is. Anyone who honors their parents with frequent communication and routine visits knows what it means to treasure their parents' role in their lives – no matter your age. It lets your parents know how much you appreciate them. It lets them know how much they mean to you. And this lets you see what kind of person they are – how selfless they are. If a person can't make time for their own parent(s), how can you expect them to make time for you when it counts?

My father routinely visited other relatives.

While my father never let anyone take him for granted, he did often visit other relatives to maintain contact. He believed in family and the way he showed that was by remaining a presence in their lives. If it was in his power to reach out, he felt that he had a responsibility to do it.

My father would readily share what he had with others.

One of the things I had the opportunity to see was how willing my father was to share what he had if he felt it could help someone else. My father loved to go to the Italian Market on 9th Street in South Philadelphia. He would load up on all kinds of fruit. Often he would buy more than we could ever eat. He would split what he had with my grandmothers, my aunts – anyone he knew. He would never take money for the goods – whatever it was. Within our family and our community, you would often hear about how my father (and mother) would give to others – the list is endless: Christmas trees to all his family and friends, Christmas toys to my cousins, handmade woodworking items. Giving is an important ingredient to leading a full life.

If my father had it to give – he'd give it.

("It" being time, money, advice, a kick-in-the-butt)

When my father saw a need, he would spring into action and do what needed to be done. He didn't have to wait to be asked or invited to help. He didn't let someone get down on their luck (as he used to say) if he could help out. He wouldn't let you get yourself into a world of trouble without telling you where you are going wrong in life and what you could do to get your life back on track. Most importantly, he would readily have his foot ready to get you in gear when your life seemed to be idling. He wanted you to stay motivated and strive to be better. One more thing that stands out for me is that he never bragged about what he did for others. He just did it. He never judged the other person as *less than* for needing a hand.

My father would take the time to talk to you, listen to you and explain things – especially to children.

My father loved to talk. Both of my parents did. I guess that's where I get it. He not only loved to talk, but he also loved to listen. Yeah, he could lecture you if that was what he felt you needed. But more often, he'd let you talk so that he too could gain insight into where your heart and mind were. My father had a wealth of knowledge just about life. He didn't go to college, but he graduated from the University of Life with a wealth of experiences to share with anyone who wanted to be enlightened.

My father required me to do well in school.

While my father didn't have experience with the inner workings of college, he instilled in me that I had to finish. I don't mean to differentiate between doing well and finishing. While in grade school and high school, doing well was what I did. But when I reached college, he saw my struggle and told me I could do it. He instilled in me early on that furthering my education was the key to a successful life. He always said that I should seek to be self-sufficient – at all times. You never wanted to be beholden to anyone. Getting my degree was the goal. Nothing less would be my best.

My father took the time to get involved in my activities and my life.

My father was involved in EVERYTHING I did. I mean everything. He went to parent/teacher conferences, recitals, girl group stuff, whatever it was. He shuttled my friends and me here and there. He drove me to and from my part-time jobs; he drove me to rehearsals – everywhere. How you support someone is by showing up – not just in a physical sense but with your heart. He believed in supporting you. So many people who knew my father always talk about how much they were helped by him getting involved in their lives.

My father would not ever let anyone disrespect him or those he loved.

I remember my father was transporting his elderly mother to his other sister's home. My grandmother was up in age and walked with a cane. She moved very slowly. We were double-parked in the street while my grandmother readied herself to get out of the car. We backed up traffic. Horns honked. People were extremely impatient. Finally, a policeman came on the scene and ordered my father to move his car RIGHT NOW. His tone was totally unsympathetic to my grandmother. My father did not hesitate in telling that police officer where to go. He said he should be ashamed of himself for not understanding that his mother was having difficulty getting out of the car. That was the kind version of the story... we were worried the officer was going to lock my father up or something. But to the contrary – the officer got out of his patrol car and proceeded to direct traffic around us until my grandmother had safely exited the vehicle and made it to the sidewalk. My father thanked the officer, and the officer apologized to my father and my grandmother.

My father had a temper but knew when it needed to be unleashed.

My father most often had to be provoked to display his temper. On several occasions, we were called the N-word as a family as we were simply on our merry way. The way it was done was always in a cowardly way – meaning it was yelled out of a passing car or as we were passing by; it was never done when there could be dialogue. This outraged my father – not to the point of harm or anything like that. I think, in hindsight, it was being powerless to change their minds, as he so liked to do. Yeah, the ignorance probably outraged him too, but my father was the kind to try to hash it out – when he could.

My father would not allow me to be exposed to things that were in conflict with his sense of wrong.

My father had a clear line dividing what he believed to be right and what he believed to be wrong. If he thought something was wrong, I was not allowed to be exposed to it. It was plain and simple. So, if a new R-rated movie was coming to town that all my friends were going to see, I was not allowed to see it – regardless of what everyone else may have been doing. I could list out so many instances where my father would tell you something is plain, and we won't be doing that or seeing that or talking about that. He would say the world is set up to do wrong so easily. Doing what's right is the hardest.

My father never said "I love you" to me – he showed me.

My father was not a touchy-feely kind of father. He never did a lot of hugging or kissing. He didn't say I love you very much either. I can tell you, though, that there was never a day that went by that I didn't know that my father loved me to the utmost. I knew it. I knew it in my heart; I knew it in my soul; I knew it in my bones. I knew it. He showed it at every opportunity he had. He showed it in the way he encouraged me. He showed it in the way he disciplined me and in the way he treated me.

My father was not afraid to let me see him cry when he lost his mother.

Honestly, I had never seen my father cry. Not until he lost his mother. I didn't know what to say. I simply hugged him. I mention this exchange because it was important for me not to equate my father's strength with never crying or feeling bad. Through that storm, he showed strength. His mother and my mother's mother, i.e., both grandmothers, passed away within two days of each other at Christmas time on Dec. 21st and Dec. 23rd of 1987. It was the strangest thing because my parents, who are always there for each other, were each in their own painful situation. My father insisted we put up our Christmas tree. He insisted we still exchange our gifts to each other. He said that emotionally – losing his mother was the toughest thing he's ever faced. But he thought it important to counter the weight of his pain with happy, joyous moments.

My father lived with no regrets.

No regrets – which shouldn't be confused with not having to say sorry if you were in the wrong. My father believed in each and every one of his decisions. If it turned out that a better alternative presented itself later, it was okay to change the course. But he believed in doing what he knew to be the best when he did it. There was no need to regret it. When he knew better, he did better. That's it. End of story.

My father found Jesus Christ and was saved.

My father always encouraged me to go to church. We were baptized at the same time. But I never really saw him take an active role in church himself. I knew he always believed in God. As he grew ill, he knew he had to do better and make sure his place in eternity was certain. He accepted Jesus Christ as his Savior. I got to see what that did in his life – albeit only for a short time. One Sunday, when we went to church, I distinctly remember one of the last sermons we got to hear together – *"To Whom Much is Given, Much is Required."* That is how I believe he always lived his life. He leaned over to me and said listen up this is important.

ABOUT THE AUTHOR

Samtra K. Devard and her husband Leonard and their three children make their home in Bear, Delaware. Samtra was born and raised in Philadelphia, Pennsylvania where she attended high school and college and enjoyed a 15 year career as a Chemical Engineer in process improvement. Samtra grew up in the church and rededicated her life to Christ in December 2008. Samtra was introduced to the subject of Christian accountability in 2009 and began the journey of accountability partnership to grow and mature in her faith in God. Little did Samtra know, the seeds of accountability were planted in her life as a young girl - by her old school Dad.

Samtra has written this book to honor her Dad and the accountability nuggets he sowed into her. Samtra belongs to Seeds of Greatness Bible Church in New Castle, DE. According to Jeremiah 29:11, God has plans to give each of us a future and a hope. Samtra believes deeply that the way to grow toward it is through accountability.

www.ingramcontent.com/pod-product-compliance
Lightning Source LLC
Chambersburg PA
CBHW031238120626
46545CB00003B/1170